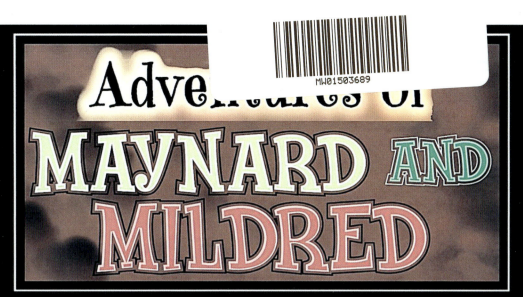

Adventures of
MAYNARD AND MILDRED

FALL STORIES

Written By

KELLY RENEE SCHUTZ

ADVENTURES OF MAYNARD AND MILDRED®

FOUR-PART SHORT-STORIED BOOK SERIES
FALL ADVENTURES

Creative Writer

KELLY RENEE SCHUTZ

Lighthearted Stories for All Ages
- SHORT STORIES -
Suitable For Ages 6-12

Featuring Puppet Narrators

Wilford	Deadward	Crazy Melmo

PUBLISHED BY
Diamond Point Entertainment, LLC, Minneapolis, Minnesota
All Rights Reserved

Maynard and Mildred® are Registered Trademarked Characters
Paranormal Universal Press, LLC

Suitable for Ages 6 to 12. Book Series = Spring, Summer, Fall, Winter.

CREATIVE WRITER
Kelly Renee Schutz

Cover Design: Ubaid Ayub and Kelly Renee Schutz
Professional Illustrator and Film Animator: Ubaid Ayub
Storywriter: Kelly Renee Schutz
Sketch Artists: Meri (Wild Creations), Brandy Woods, Bilal Haider
Pictorial and Artistic Illustrations: Aqsa Sarwar, Mehak Fatima, and Creative Commons
Puppet (Trademarked): by Voicing Things (Wilford), United Kingdom
Puppets (Trademarked): by Andy Clinton (Deadward and Crazy Melmo), United States
Content Editors and/or Pen Names: Abigail Frank, Eva Palmer

Hardcover Fall Adventures (2025): ISBN: 979-8-319-49178-7
Paperback Fall Adventures (2025): ISBN: 979-8-319-49112-1
First Version Screenplay Paperback (2018): ISBN-13: 978-1-984-09273-1
Library of Congress Control Number (2018): 2018933902
UPC Code (Audio CD) (2018): 191091581018

Kindle Direct Publishing, an Amazon.com Company
Printed in the United States of America
(Copyright 2025)

TABLE OF CONTENTS
ADVENTURES OF MAYNARD AND MILDRED®

FALL ADVENTURES - 8 Short Stories
September, October, November

<u>Dedication</u>

To my husband for his support
in my need to be creative.
Together, our memories are replicated in
the lives of
"Maynard and Mildred".

Adventures of Maynard and Mildred®

 MAYNARD

MILDRED

CHARACTERS

Dr. Kelly created *Maynard and Mildred*® in 2016. She and Dr. Michael scripted and voiced the roles of *Maynard and Mildred*® for an audiobook published in 2018. In 2025, she modified the original from "Maynard and Mildred: Comedic Adventures" to "Adventures of Maynard and Mildred." The stories within the four-part series are being produced into a short, animated film.

IMAGINARY FRIENDS

From an early age, children are introduced to an imaginary world. Some are given dolls or action heroes to play with while others are seated in front of a television where active, colorful cartoons or imaginative characters come to life entertaining them. Before the age of 14, many children seek the company of one or more imaginary friends. Pretending to interact with an invisible playmate is healthy and enhances different developmental skills.

MAYNARD CREATES MILDRED

It began when Maynard was raised as an only child. Mildred, his imaginary friend, came to life when his parents moved around a lot. Maynard found it difficult making friends in school so he created Mildred to keep him company. Through his many life adventures, Mildred helped Maynard become more independent, outgoing, confident, patient, problem-solving, lighthearted, entertained, spontaneous, and comfortable adjusting to alone time.

***

FALL
ADVENTURES

***

STORY 1
FIELD TRIP NATURE FARM

It was the month of October. A month that signaled to students that an out-of-classroom field trip was about to occur. Experiential exploration, otherwise known as hands-on learning, is how the teachers would describe the activity.

As the excitement heightened, the energy could be felt in every corner of the school grounds. Students of all ages would gather to suggest ideas for their annual class trips. As a learning tool, teachers suggested students use thought strategies to narrow ideas for their day of exploration.

Once ideas were submitted, a class vote would honor the activity. This year, Maynard's class voted to visit a nature farm. A nature farm would bring experiences he would not normally get living in a small-town, city atmosphere.

Going out into the country opened the senses to welcoming experiences. The country was an environment filled with various smells, cool breezes, noisy animals, and exploration.

Getting ready and out the door for school was the same ole, same ole, for Maynard.

Every day, he would drag himself out of bed, rush to put his clothes on, grab his toast smeared with peanut butter and jam, and shove the front door open rushing out of the house.

"See yah later, Mom!" he would yell, chewing on a half piece of toast spread with globs of messy goodness left on his face.

"Maynard, why are you in such a hurry every morning?" she said. "And stop inhaling your toast. You will choke. Here is a wet rag, wipe your face! Geezz, that boy, … what will people think of my parenting skills?"   3

"Not running, Mom … walking quickly," he would shout back. "I need to catch the school bus. Today, we are going on a field trip to Red Pine Nature Farm. How exciting!"

"Be careful Maynard," his mother said. "Last time you went on a nature farm trip, you fell into a pond. Be mindful and stay with your tour guide and classmates. And, don't go putting your hand directly into the mouth of a farm animal."

Maynard's mother always had an over-protective side of her. But she did make a good point. Maynard seemed to find himself getting tangled up in situations no matter where he went.

As the school bus approached Maynards stop, he could hear its brakes squeak [rumble-squeak-rumble]. Hesitating for a moment, he would proceed with caution as he walked up the steps into the bus. A scent of exhaust fumes would drift toward him notably coming from the bus's rusty tailpipe.

"Whoa! Those exhaust fumes are strong this morning Mr. bus driver," he would remark.

"I'll get that looked at Maynard. Thanks for letting me know," the bus driver remarked. "Maynard, this morning we are going directly to the nature farm."

"Yippee!" he said. Maynard took his usual seat in the front row sitting next to the window. The squeaky door closed. The bus continued picking up the rest of his classmates while making its way down a long, gravel road to the nature farm.

SCREECH!! [the bus coming to a stop]

The sound of its rusty brakes could be heard a mile away. The bus stopped in front of the gate of Red Pine Nature Farm.

Along the way to the farm, as Maynard looked out the window, he couldn't help but notice how pretty the countryside was with its rolling hills and farm animals scattered about. He even noticed nature trails.

The bus stopped at the Red Pine Nature farm gate. "Have a good day, kids! Enjoy your nature farm experience!" the bus driver shouted.

The students, one-by-one, were buzzing with energy. As they hopped off the bus, their breath could be seen in the chilly air.

The crisp autumn air carried with it a scent of dew kissed fallen leaves and fresh hay. Golden, red, and orange leaves

carpeted the ground, dried to the touch, crunching beneath excited footsteps. A nearby pond, deep blue in color, glistened with sparkles.

"This is going to be amazing!" Maynard grinned, holding his lunch bag tightly. "Feeding the animals and exploring nature? Count me in!"

Beyond the gate, the tour guide awaited the class. "Come on over here everyone!" the tour guide shouted.

As Maynard positioned himself in the front row of the group, Mildred neared him. Her translucent body gleamed faintly under the morning sun.

"Hello, Maynard," she said. "A farm, huh?"

"I bet you will hear talking cows and be pestered by chickens plotting pranks," she giggled. "Maybe even a wise old rooster will give you some advice."

"Holy nature farm, Mildred," Maynard mumbled. "What are you doing here? You will scare away all the animals."

"I'm here to keep you company and a watchful eye on you," Mildred whispered. "Besides, who else would you rather share this experience with?"

Maynard shouted, "Me, myself, and myself!"

His outburst caused the classmates and tour guide to turn around looking in his direction.

Maynard's face turned bright red. He went silent.

"Never mind," he said. "Sorry about that. I have a habit of talking to myself out loud. I'll be quiet."

Unusual glances from every direction remained on Maynard.

"Okay everyone. Follow me in this direction," said the tour guide. "Let me remind you that when we get to the barn, we must remain quiet. Some of the animals are sleeping."

As they followed their tour guide, Maynard felt the thrill of adventure bubbling inside him.

Red Pine Nature Farm promised a day filled with new experiences. With Mildred by his side, there was no telling what kind of farmyard fun awaited them.

"And, here we are at our first stop," the tour guide said. "We are at the goat petting center."

Maynard and his classmates gathered eagerly around the wooden fence of the petting area. The cheerful sounds of goats made noises that filled the air.

"Look everyone (pointing), … look over there! There is a goat chewing on trash," a classmate shouted.

Giggles erupted from the students.

"I wonder if that goat has a name," someone shouted. "Let's call the goat … *Tin Can Billy*!" The classmates giggled.

"Hey, everyone, look over here," said Maynard. "I think a sheep is coming over to greet us. Look, it has a red knitted scarf around its neck. That's so cool! Hello SHEEP!"

A fluffy white sheep came over to the fence and nuzzled Maynard's outstretched hand as he sprinkled feed from a small brown bag onto the ground.

"Hey! His mouth is tickling my hand," he laughed.

"This is amazing!" Maynard grinned, marveling at how gentle the animal was.

Hovering just above the fence, Mildred inspected a bright-red rooster strutting proudly in the nearby enclosure. "Well, aren't you the boss of this place?" she chuckled. "Hey, do you speak Rooster'ish?"

The rooster tilted its head, looking at Mildred, giving her a wink before it clucked and walked away.

Mildred flapped her arms like wings and let out a series of what she thought were convincing chicken clucks.

"Cluck-cluck-ca-caw!" she said.

The rooster responded with a piercing crow, as if declaring a challenge. Startled, the goats scattered, and a few sheep trotted nervously toward the back of the pen.

"Oops," Mildred muttered.

"Seriously, Mildred?" Maynard whispered, glancing nervously at the bewildered farmhand nearby. "Do you always have to cause a scene?"

Mildred grinned mischievously. "I was just making my introductions to the farm animals."

Maynard sighed, brushing hay off his jeans. "Can we just keep this more relaxed? Please?"

"Here we have our beautiful nature trail," the tour guide said. "Do not wander off of it because you never know what lurks in the forest area."

Maynard and his classmates followed each other down a long, winding nature trail.

Through the wooded forest, he noticed and pointed out golden, red, and amber leaves falling from the trees. At times, he would reach out to grab a few floating in the air near him.

The leaves that had fallen on the trail made a crackling sound and crunch as the classmates stepped on top of them.

CRUNCH-CRUNCH-CRUNCH.

Suddenly, Mildred gasped. "Look, Maynard, ... is that a blue butterfly? It is so pretty, look how blue it is!" she exclaimed, pointing at it as it sat on a leaf. I need to take a closer look."

Maynard glanced at the group. He looked back at the deep woods. His mind began to wander as he was also intrigued by the flutter of the blue butterfly.

"Uh, Maynard," Mildred said. "Don't start wandering off. The tour guide told us to stay with the group." But it was too late.

Maynard began walking toward the deep woods so he could get a closer look at the butterfly.

"No worries, Maynard," said Mildred. "I will get the butterfly and bring it back to you so you can see it. I will be back before anyone notices we have drifted off," she remarked.

Maynard sighed and dashed after her. "Mildred! Come back!" he called, pushing aside branches as he tried to keep up.

In his rush to catch up with Mildred, Maynard didn't see two piles of damp leaves ahead. His foot slipped, and with a loud "Whoa!" he landed right on one of its piles. Mud splattered all over him.

Mildred turned around, eyes wide with concern. "Oh no! Maynard, are you okay?"

Maynard wiped mud from his face, trying not to laugh at the ridiculousness of the situation. "I've been better," he said.

"Mr. Maynard!" shouted the tour guide. "Where are you? You are not supposed to wander off the trail into the woods. Please get back here!"

As Maynard returned to the group, one of his classmates started to tease him. "You look like you had a mud fight." [ha-ha-ha]

Maynard sheepishly chuckled. "You could say that."

"Class, we are now off the nature trail and entering our spectacular pumpkin patch," shouted the tour guide. "Be careful where you are stepping. The pumpkins do not like to be stepped on."

The class eagerly entered the patch, eyes wide open at the sight of plump orange pumpkins scattered across the field.

"And, you may pick a small pumpkin to bring home with you. So, pick wisely!" the tour guide shouted out.

Maynard surveyed the patch, searching for the perfect pumpkin. "That one!" as he pointed to a bright, round one, near the edge of a wagon.

13

Mildred neared glancing mischievously at a tall stack of pumpkins that were piled on a nearby wagon. "Maynard, I think you should pick this small one at the bottom. Here let me help you!"

With a playful nudge, Mildred pulled the small pumpkin from the bottom of the pile causing the other pumpkins on top to fall onto the ground.

"UT-OH. WATCH OUT below!" Mildred screamed. "Avalanche!"

The pumpkins made a loud noise as they tumbled off the wagon and onto the ground. Pumpkins rolled in every direction, bumping into students and scattering across the field.

The class erupted in laughter and shouted, "Watch out!" Classmates darted away from the wagon.

Heart pounding, Maynard rushed to the scene. "I'm so sorry," as he apologized to the nature farm owner.

"I'm in trouble now," Maynard gasped.

"Maynard," said the farm owner. "Why don't you help me pick these pumpkins up and we can just call this an accident waiting to happen."

Maynard looked at the farm owner, his tour guide, and classmates with horror in his eyes.

Suddenly, the tour guide and classmates started to clap.

"Good job, buddy," shouted a classmate. "Yeah, close call Maynard but at least you are not hurt," said the tour guide.

They all pitched in and helped the farm owner place the pumpkins back onto the wagon.

As the day at Red Pine Nature Farm ended, Maynard and Mildred sat quietly on a grassy hill, gazing out at the sunset.

The chaos of the day—Maynard falling in the forest while on the nature trail, and, the tumbling pumpkins from the wagon, made him think about his day in reflection.

"You know, Maynard," said Mildred. "Farms are fun. They are full of adventures and surprises. But they also remind us that nature demands care and respect. Sometimes, our excitement gets the best of us, and we end up causing a bit of unexpected situations."

Maynard nodded slowly. "I guess you're right Mildred. Today was crazy, but I learned that even when things don't go as planned, staying calm and working together can turn what appears to be a mess into something fun."

Mildred smiled warmly. "Exactly. And sometimes, all you need is a bit of teamwork and a positive attitude to make a day memorable."

"Time to get back onto the bus," shouted the tour guide.

And with a rush, the classmates loaded the bus one-by-one, most of them pushing each other aside to get to the back row seats.

As the bus pulled slowly away from the gate of Red Pine Nature Farm, the sound of laughter filled the inside of the bus. Yes, you could say, the sounds of an annual school exploration trip, fulfilled its promise to help students learn and explore … the best nature could provide.

***

"IMAGINATION" HELPS YOU BECOME LESS STRESSED AND MORE CARING.

***

"WILFORD"
THIS STORY CONTINUES

AHHH ... YES ...

Annual school learning trips. Those were the days, weren't they?

I remember a time when my 2nd grade class went on a field trip to a bubble gum factory.

There must have been twenty different flavors of bubble gum. And, I wanted to try every single one of them.

Well, we were told to take one gum sample, but I decided to sneak five gum samples and put all of them into my mouth.

You could say my mouth was a bit full.

I was chewing on all of them at once when my teacher noticed and came over to me and said, "spit it out."

Out of my mouth and into her hand came this HUGE wad of gums - yellow, green, pink, and purple – all bound together like a knitted sweater.

My teacher looked at the gum wad in her hand, looked at me, and with a murmur said ... "eeewww" ... her face must has turned three shades of green.

Ah, yes, those were the good ole days.

EXCEPT,
Speaking of mixing things together ...
There was that one time in baking class ...

STORY 2
BAKING CLASS

"Maynard, hurry up, you will be late for your cookie baking class," shouted his mother.

"One second Mom. I am washing my hands," he replied.

As his mother drove him to their local community center, Maynard couldn't help but ramble on with excitement. After all, today was the day he would be learning how to bake a perfect batch of chocolate chip cookies.

The community center was a short distance from his house. "Maynard, you have a good time today" his mother said.

"See yah later, Mom," he shouted back. "I'm going to bring home the best tasting chocolate chip cookies EVER."

Maynard walked into the building. A lady wearing a knitted hat awaited him while sitting at her desk. "Check-in is right here," she said. "Name young man?" she asked.

"Maynard," he replied. "I am here for the chocolate chip cookie baking class. I'm going to learn how to make a perfect batch of chocolate chip cookies."

"You certainly sound determined," the lady said. "You have a good time today."

As Maynard was making his way down a long hallway to the community center kitchen, he could hear the baking instructor talking.

"And when you perfect our chocolate chip cookie baking class today, you will be invited back to make Christmas cookies," said the baking instructor.

The participants buzzed with excitement.

The community center kitchen rattled noisily with participants of all ages anxiously scrambling around, bumping into each other, attempting to find their spots at various baking posts.

The warm, inviting aroma of sugar, butter, and spices, greeted Maynard as he walked into the kitchen. "WOW!" he said.

The air was filled with a glimpse of what was yet to be baked. His eyes widened as he looked at all the baking equipment and ingredients sitting on the countertops.

"What would you like to master today young man," said the baking instructor.

Maynard clutched a well-worn recipe book he brought from home. He dreamed of creating the perfect batch of chocolate chip cookies.

"Today, I'm going to be mastering the perfect chocolate chip cookie Ms. instructor!"

As he took his position at his baking post, a familiar, playful voice echoed through the room.

"Hello Maynard," said the voice.

"Holy cookie, Mildred," he mumbled. "What are you doing here? I am here to learn how to make a perfect chocolate chip cookie. I can't have you hanging around me as I am perfecting my work. This work requires pure concentration."

"I'm here assist you and to keep you company, Maynard," she said. "I can help you with a few of my baking skills to spice things up," she teased.

"AH, no thanks," he replied. "I am here to become a master chocolate chip cookie baker! No girls or assistance allowed."

As participants were about to grab a mixing bowl, the instructor, Mrs. Baker, entered the room.

Mrs. Baker was known for her exceptional baking tips and for winning blue ribbons at county and state fairs. She stood by the stove, stepped forward, and introduced herself to the class.

"Alright, class, today we're going to learn the basics of baking!" she announced. "And, today, we are going to start with the art of measuring."

With practiced ease, Mrs. Baker demonstrated how to measure ingredients precisely, mix the dough to just the right consistency, and preheat the oven to the perfect temperature.

Maynard listened intently, scribbling notes in his little recipe book as he tried to capture every detail.

As Mrs. Baker poured flour into a large mixing bowl, Mildred neared, her eyes gleaming with mischief.

"You know, Maynard," she quipped in her quirky tone, "a dash of magic never hurt anyone. Maybe I should help you and sprinkle a little fairy dust into that bowl!"

"AH, no thanks, Mildred," said Maynard. "Besides, I don't want my chocolate chip cookies to be sprinkled with fairy dust. I want my cookies to be a Maynard special."

"Did you say something young man?" asked Mrs. Baker. "Are you asking me a question?"

"AH, no Ma'am, I mean Mrs. Baker," mumbled Maynard. "I tend to talk to myself out of habit. Sorry, I'll be quiet."

His comment made a few of the other participants giggle, though Maynard frowned and focused harder on Mrs. Baker's instructions.

"Be quiet, Mildred," he said. "You are going to get me in trouble and kicked out of here."

Mildred continued to hover near Maynard. She offered him offbeat tips such as, "Mix your ingredients like you're stirring up one of you mud patties!"

"Mildred, be quiet. I'm not making a mud patty," he remarked. "I'm making the perfect chocolate chip cookie."

The room went silent. Maynard's slipped comment about comparing his chocolate chip cookie dough to a mud patty was heard out loud causing the participants to burst out in laughter.

Maynard turned beat red in his face. "Ah, sorry, I'm talking to myself again."

Though mildly exasperated by Mildred's antics, Maynard couldn't help but smile at the infectious energy spreading throughout the room.

The combination of careful instruction, friendly chatter, and Mildred's whimsical observations turned the lesson into a lively, communal experience—one that promised not only delicious treats but also the joy of learning together.

Maynard gathered his ingredients and prepared to mix his dough with careful precision. As he began to stir his ingredients, Mildred neared him closer.

She had a mischievous glint in her eye. "Maynard, you need a little magic in that mix!" she declared, and with a playful flick of her wrist, she disturbed the bowl.

In an instant, a glob of dough splattered across the countertop, and a few dollops of flour soared into the air like snow.

Maynard's carefully measured ingredients went wildly off track, and the dough transformed into a messy, lumpy concoction that refused to turn into a dough-like glob.

"Uh-oh," Maynard muttered, his cheeks flushing with embarrassment as he tried desperately to salvage his batch. The chaos intensified when the oven timer beeped, and he hurriedly scooped up what he could manage.

"Maynard, I think the cookies need to bake for 12 minutes," Mildred observed.

"Mildred, these cookies need more time because they are bigger," he mumbled.

When Maynard pulled the cookie sheet out of the oven, the cookies turned out flat and uneven, with a few burnt edges peeking out from the dough.

"YUCK," shouted Mildred. "Start over."

Participants burst into laughter and playful teasing. "Maynard, it looks like your dough is trying to form its very own masterpiece!" Mildred giggled. She compared the scene to a "snowy art project."

Frustration and embarrassment washed over Maynard. He wondered if he should just give up on baking altogether. But amid the laughter and the good-natured ribbing from his participant friends, he felt a spark of determination.

The friendly atmosphere reminded him that mistakes were part of learning, and that even the messiest mishaps could lead to delicious discoveries if he kept trying.

With a deep breath and a determined nod, Maynard resolved to fix his recipe, proving that even a baking blunder could be turned into a steppingstone toward success.

After the initial baking blunder, the instructor stepped in with a warm smile and a quick demonstration on how to salvage a recipe gone awry. "Don't worry, everyone," Mrs. Baker said, showing them how to gently fold in the ingredients and adjust the baking time.

Inspired by her guidance, Maynard gathered his ingredients once more, his eyes bright with determination.

"Come on Maynard," said Mildred. "No time to give up. Start over and perfect your cookie!"

This time, Maynard worked with a careful focus that he hadn't mustered before. He measured each ingredient precisely, mixed the dough slowly, and even double-checked his recipe.

The class watched as Maynard arranged his cookie dough on the baking tray and slid it into the heated oven.

After 20 minutes baking, the cookies emerged looking imperfect again—each one slightly uneven, with a few quirks that made them uniquely his. Some cookies were a tad crisper on the edges, while others retained a soft, chewy center.

"Getting there," he shouted. "I am going to try this one more time."

A round of cheers erupted from both the instructor and his classmates. "That's the spirit, Maynard!" Mrs. Baker exclaimed.

Mildred neared him with a playful grin, teasing, "I must say, your abstract baking style is truly one-of-a-kind. Kudos for not giving up!"

Maynard smiled broadly, the warmth of success and the support around him filling him with pride. The big reveal had turned chaos into creativity, proving that perseverance and teamwork could turn even a baking mishap into a delightful victory.

After his third attempt, the kitchen began to quiet down as the last of the laughter subsided. Participants were cleaning up their stations and leaving.

Maynard lingered for a moment, cleaning up his workstation, and took a deep breath to reflect on the day's baking adventure.

His thoughts swirled as he recalled every slip, every splatter, and every burst of laughter. "Even if my cookies aren't perfect, I learned something valuable today," he mused.

"Persistence and learning from mistakes matter more than just getting it right the first time."

"Maynard," said Mrs. Baker. "You did a very good job today perfecting your chocolate chip cookie recipe. May I suggest more butter and less salt next time?"

Mildred neared. "Maynard, I have to admit," she said quietly, "I like your determination to make the perfect cookie."

Maynard gathered his things, walked out of the kitchen, and headed down the hallway toward the door. His mother was waiting patiently for him.

As he walked outside, he carried with him a plate of 12 chocolate chip cookies. Some burnt, some mushy, some crisp.

"What do you have here Maynard," his mother asked. "Are these your masterpiece chocolate chip cookies?"

"You bet Mom," said Maynard. "I'm still in my learning stages."

"They look marvelous dear," she said.

"Would you like one?" Maynard asked.

"Well, certainly," she said. "Which one would you like me to pick?"

"Here, you can have this one. It is less burnt, a little soft, and a lot of chewy," he said. "Do you like it?"

"Well, it sure tastes good Maynard," as she took a small bite. "Yummy."

"WHEW, Maynard, I think I am going to take off," said Mildred. "Have fun eating your burnt cookies. Maybe next time, you should take note of Mrs. Baker's suggestion and add more butter and reduce some salt. Why don't we call your cookies – "Maynard's Magnificent Cookies!"

***

"IMAGINATION"
HELPS
YOU BECOME A
BETTER
PROBLEM SOLVER.

***

STORY 3
AMUSEMENT PARK

"Hurry up Mom and Dad," shouted Maynard, as he rushed out of the house to get into their family car. "I can't WAIT to get to the amusement park! I'm going to play games and go on a ride called, "Hurricane Maximum."

"Slow down, Maynard," shouted his mother. "We need to finish a few things here first. It is going to be a very long day."

As his parents drove to the amusement park, Maynard, who sat in the backseat, pressed his face up against the car window feeling the warmth of the sun on his face as he tingled with anticipation and energy.

His parents arrived at the amusement park pulling into a parking space. Maynard could hardly sit still in his seat. When the car came to a dead stop, he jumped out. Stretching his arms into the air, he could feel a sense of unsettled energy and hear festive music within the confines of the park.

"Three tickets please," Maynard requested to the ticket clerk. "This is so great, once you get inside, all the rides are FREE!"

"Mom and Dad, see yah later," shouted Maynard. "I am going to head in this direction toward the rides."

"Now, you be careful, Maynard," warned his mother. "If you get lost, find someone who works at this park to help you find us. And don't lose your hat like you did last time. Keep an eye on it."

Maynard waved at his parents as they parted in separate directions. He pressed his baseball cap down on his head to assure it was not going to fall off.

"Let's do this," he mumbled to himself.

Maynard was excited. He could smell the irresistible scent of popcorn and cotton candy mingling with the crisp autumn breeze. He stopped for a moment to assess his situation.

Everywhere he looked, colorful rides soared high against a clear blue sky, and the bustling crowd added to the atmosphere of joyful anticipation.

Maynard's heart raced with excitement as he took in the sight of looping roller coasters and spinning teacups. Although thrilled by the promise of games and prizes, he couldn't shake a hint of nervousness about the more daring attractions.

"I'm ready for an adventure," he thought, imagining a day full of fun, laughter, and maybe even a few harmless thrills.

Just then, a familiar, mischievous voice broke through his thoughts. "Hello Maynard," said an excited voice.

"Holy pull a ducky game, ... Mildred," mumbled Maynard.

"What are you doing here?" he asked. "I am looking for the roller coaster ride *Hurricane Maximum*. It slowly goes up a tall slope and then, at the top, it twists and turns as it rushes with top speed to the bottom WOW!".

"Sounds dangerous, Maynard." remarked Mildred. "Are you sure you are of the right height to do that ride?"

"I think so," Maynard commented. "They have a height chart by the ride. I look tall for my age. Besides, they wouldn't have this ride if it was *that* dangerous."

"Let's go and make this day unforgettable Mildred!" Maynard shouted. "There it is! WOW!"

Maynard's eyes widened as he stared at the towering roller coaster, its tracks twisting in a dizzying loop. Despite his nerves, he felt a surge of determination to take his first ride.

"I'm going to try this," he declared, stepping toward the ride.

"Maynard," Mildred said, as she pointed to the height chart. "Is that the height chart?"

Maynard walked over to the chart to measure his height. As his back lay against the wall, he used his finger to rest on top of it to mark his height.

"WHOA," he said. "I barely made it."

The thrill of the ride continued to beckon him as his heart pounded. He stood in line with taller kids waiting his turn to ride.

"Kid, you are too short for this ride," smirked a taller kid who stood in front of him.

Mildred neared beside Maynard with a smirk on her face. "Maynard, pay no attention to that boy. You met the height restriction so let's do this."

"Maybe I shouldn't," Maynard said, as his stomach gurgled while his knees went weak.

"Mildred, this might be a bad idea. What if that kid is right. I barely met the height restrictions," he remarked.

"Oh, come on, Maynard! This is where the real fun begins!" she teased. "Just imagine the wind in your hair and the scream on your face—sounds spectacular, doesn't it?" Her playful tone did little to ease his anxiety, but it did spark a hint of excitement.

"NEXT!" shouted the amusement ride operator. "Sit yourself right here."

Once seated in the roller coaster car, Maynard clutched the safety bar as the ride slowly ascended. The panoramic view of the park, with its vibrant colors and bustling crowd, made him momentarily forget his fear. But just as he began to relax, the ride jolted into motion with a sudden lurch.

At that moment, Mildred couldn't resist her signature antics. Nearing the front of the amusement car, she began mimicking the sound of the coaster—an over-the-top, comical "Wheeeeee!" that sent the car into a fit of giggles from some nearby riders. Startled, Maynard's grip tightened so much that his hat flew off, spiraling into the air.

"Hey! My hat!" he shouted, his voice a mix of exhilaration and panic. His cheeks flushed red as he awkwardly reached out, trying to grab it while the coaster dipped and swirled.

Between the abrupt drops of the roller coaster, Maynard's emotions ran high—one moment he was laughing at the thrill, the next he was cringing at his own clumsy reaction.

Mildred's teasing remarks about his cautious nature only added to the humorous tension, leaving Maynard both embarrassed and oddly proud of his daredevil spirit.

The ride ended in a brisk jolt. Maynard jumped off and started walking away. "WOW!" he screamed, looking back at *Hurricane Maximum*.

The ride operator approached him and returned his hat that flew off during the ride.

"Thanks Mr. ride operator," Maynard said. "WOW! What a great ride! I will have to tell my parents to go on it."

After the adrenaline of the roller coaster ride began to fade, Maynard and Mildred strolled over to the colorful rows of game booths lining the amusement park walkways.

The air buzzed with laughter and the clinking of prizes as kids of all ages tried their luck at the water balloon game, the ducky pulling game, and the ring toss.

Maynard's eyes sparkled with determination as he approached the ducky in the water pulling game. "Rabbits," he said. "I lost. I pulled a ducky that gave me a plastic ring. I'll try my hand at the ring toss booth. I feel a huge stuffed animal coming my way.

"I'm going to win me that HUGE bear hanging above my head," Maynard declared, signing up for the challenge with a mix of confidence and nerves. He gripped a handful of plastic rings and stepped up to the booth.

The bottles stood neatly arranged on the table, looking shiny under the tent lights. Maynard focused intently on a bottle standing in the center that became his target.

But before he could toss his first ring, Mildred intervened in her usual quirky manner. As she hovered over Maynard's shoulders, she whispered, "Watch this, Maynard."

Mischievously, she tapped one of the bottles with her invisible fingers. "See that Maynard," she commented.

To Maynard's surprise, the bottle wobbled slightly—so much that the rings thrown at it bounced off its bottle neck rim and flew off in multiple directions.

CLINK-CLINK-CLINK.

One ring sailed wildly and clanged against a side wall; another ricocheted off a bottle, narrowly missing a nearby participant's head. Laughter erupted from the small crowd that had gathered, and Maynard's cheeks flushed as he fumbled with his remaining rings.

"Maybe I'm just not cut out for this," he muttered.

"Here Maynard," shouted Mildred. "Let me help you!"

Mildred couldn't contain her enthusiasm to help Maynard win a large stuffed teddy bear. "Time for some action, Maynard."

"WHOA … look at all those rings dance," Maynard shouted.

"Here Maynard," shouted Mildred. "Throw a few rings now."

Maynard tossed three rings in different directions and one caught on the rim of a bottle with a yellow tipped color.

"I did it," shouted Maynard. "I'm a WINNER!"

Onlookers noticed the bottles were wiggling as Maynard threw the rings and began accusing the game operator of rigging the game.

"Must be the wind because those bottles never move," the game operator, who stood there puzzled, remarked back.

In the end, despite Maynard's greatest effort and Mildred's help, no large stuffed teddy bear was won that day. Maynard failed to land a single ring on the bottle target. The vendor handed him a consolation prize—"here you go pal," the operator said. "This is the best I can give you - a small, plastic superhero toy."

Maynard looked at the toy and said, "Who is it? I don't even recognize the action figure."

"Kid, I just hand out the prizes, I don't have to know what I am handing out," said the game operator. "Now run along."

Maynard held onto the action figure as he walked back in the direction of the ticket booth.

He had had an exciting day despite almost losing his hat while riding *Hurricane Maximum*, winning an unrecognizable superhero toy at a ring toss game, and eating a hot dog, cotton candy, elephant ear, and drinking three sodas – he was feeling gross with an upset stomach and ready to go home.

"I feel gross," he mumbled. "What a great day!"

"WHEW," said Mildred. "Maynard, I am going to take off. You have had an exciting day today. I'm glad you didn't get hurt while riding *Hurricane Maximum*. I am sure there will be a write-up in the newspaper tomorrow about games at amusement parks being rigged. And, to think, I won't be getting any credit for that. And, recover from all the food you have eaten. I am sure you must have a big stomachache."

Maynard spotted his mother and father near the booth and waved as he approached them.

"What do we have here?" his father said, as he took the plastic superhero from Maynard's hand.

"I won it at the ring toss. An action hero, Dad," Maynard said.

"Who is it?" asked his father. "I've never seen this character before. Is it a new action hero?"

"I don't think so dad," Maynard replied. Maynard knew it was a cheap look-alike of "*Zippy the Motorcycle Man.*" He changed the subject.

As they left the amusement park heading toward the parking lot, Maynard couldn't help but study the look of the superhero.

"Maybe Mildred is right," he said to himself. "Maybe this superhero won its way into spending more time with me. Maybe he too, was looking for a friend."

And, with a smile on his face, he buckled himself into the back seat of the car and fell asleep as his parents drove him home.

Maynard had indeed had, a great day at the amusement park.

"CRAZY MELMO"
THIS STORY CONTINUES

YEE-HAHHH ... Crazy Melmo here.

Looks to me, ... Maynard had an eventful day at the amusement park.

Maynard, ... you may not have won yourself a BIG stuffed animal but you sure won a few memories ... pull a ducky and win a plastic ring. He-he-he. Was it pink?

How many people can say they have ever kept their plastic ring? I did once. That was until my dog chewed on it and accidentally swallowed it.

When it came out the other end ... it wasn't a ring anymore. Looked more like a ... well ... you can only imagine.

YEE-HAHHH ...

And, the last time I took a ride on *Hurricane Maximum*, my false teeth fell out of my mouth and hit the "ring the bell" game. Man thought I cheated. Not with those choppers.

I won a *long glowing stick*. Not just any stick. It glowed all kinds of bright colors. People would stop me just to admire it. You bet. I was so honored carrying that thing around. Until the glow faded to black ... YEE-NOTHING.

I wanted to get rid of it. All the waste baskets said, "DO NOT THROW what use to be a *long glow stick* in this basket!"

Now people were laughing at me holding this dull stick ... Speaking of stuff on a stick, Maynard went to a county fair one time ...

44

STORY 4
COUNTY FAIR

The annual county fair was finally here, and Maynard could barely contain his excitement.

"See yah later, Mom and Dad," Maynard shouted. "I'm heading over to the county fair to see the animals, go on a few rides, eat my way through it, and win a big prize!"

"Don't eat too much before you go on some of those crazy rides, Maynard," his mother yelled. "You know what happened last time. You were sick for days."

As Maynard entered the county fairgrounds, he could not help but stop and admire the bright streamers and flashing lights that decorated what lay beyond the gate.

While entering, he could smell roasted corn, popcorn, and funnel cakes drifting through the air.

The cheerful jingles from carnival games and the mechanical hum of rides blended with the delighted SCREAMS of fairgoers on the roller coaster rides.

Maynard approached the ticket counter, purchased tickets, and proceeded to walk down the lane of games. "This is going to be the best day ever! I'm going to win the biggest stuffed bear and eat a mountain of cotton candy!"

Suddenly, a familiar voice approached him. "Did someone say cotton candy?" Mildred, his invisible friend, materialized beside him.

"WHOA!" she said. "Look at the size of that cotton candy on a stick! It's like someone took a rainbow and spun it around into a big ball!" Mildred exclaimed.

"Behave, Mildred," Maynard warned, already bracing himself for trouble. "We don't want to get kicked out of here."

Mildred pretended to look innocent, clasping her hands behind her back. "Relax, Maynard. I'm here for the fun. And maybe a giant stuffed animal or two!"

As they strolled around the fairgrounds, their first stop was to see the animals in the barns.

"Look Maynard," Mildred shouted in enthusiasm. "I see ducks, chickens, bunnies, and *moooo*, a great big cow!"

"Mildred, that's not a cow!" Maynard reacted. "What you are looking at is the world's largest pig! COOL! And, it's eating snacks! Look, the sign says – "Don't Feed Me. I Am Picky About The Types Of Snacks I Like To Eat."

As they left the barns, they strolled past the game booths. Mildred spotted a ring toss game. Her eyes lit up. "That one!" she declared, pointing. "Let's win a massive teddy bear!"

"It's not that easy," Maynard replied.

"EASY sneezy," Mildred insisted, grabbing a ring from the counter. "I could win this blindfolded. Watch!"

The cheerful music of the carnival games lured Maynard and Mildred closer to a brightly colored booth with a giant sign that read "Win Big! Giant Prizes!" Behind the counter stood a grinning vendor in a striped shirt, spinning a ring on his finger.

"This is it," Mildred said, her eyes glued to the massive teddy bear hanging above the booth. "That bear is coming home with us, Maynard!"

Maynard handed one of his tickets to the carnival vendor and picked up a ring. The bottles glistened under the carnival lights, looking deceptively close together. He squinted, aimed, and tossed the ring. It sailed through the air and... bounced right off the rim of a bottle.

"Try again, kid!" the vendor said with a smirk.

Maynard tried two more times, each ring bouncing off the bottles in frustratingly unpredictable directions. He sighed. "This is impossible!"

Mildred neared closer, narrowing her eyes. "Impossible, my foot! This thing is rigged, Maynard! Look at those bottles they're probably glued together!"

"I'm pretty sure they're not," Maynard whispered, glancing nervously at the vendor.

"Step aside, amateur." Mildred grabbed one of the rings and, using her "invisible powers," tilted one of the bottles slightly.

Maynard's jaw dropped. "Mildred, no!"

The ring sailed through the air, clinking perfectly onto the neck of the bottle. The vendor blinked, confused.

"Winner, winner, chicken dinner," shouted Maynard.

"I demand the bear!" Mildred declared dramatically.

Before Maynard could protest, the vendor shrugged, handed over a tiny plastic keychain instead, and muttered, "No guarantees on size, kid."

"Rabbits," Maynard groaned. Mildred spotted another game with a strength tester. "Let's go over to this game," she said.

"You've got this one, Maynard!" Mildred said, pointing at the towering contraption with a bell at the top.

"Are you sure? I'm not that strong," Maynard hesitated, eyeing the oversized mallet.

"Pfft, strength is overrated. Just swing the hammer and let me handle the rest," Mildred said confidently.

Maynard reluctantly picked up the mallet, gripping it tightly. He swung with all his might, but just as the mallet was about to hit the lever, Mildred decided to "help." She grabbed the mallet mid-swing and yanked it upward, throwing off his balance.

The mallet soared through the air and landed in a nearby cotton candy stand with a loud *thud*. Pink clouds of cotton candy puffed into the air as the vendor yelled, "Hey! Watch it!"

Maynard turned bright red, while Mildred doubled over laughing. "Well, that was unexpected!" she said between giggles.

"I told you not to 'help'!" Maynard groaned, hiding his face as the cotton candy vendor glared at them.

"Maynard, let's get out of here," said Mildred. "We know when our fun is not appreciated."

Maynard and Mildred continued wandering through the carnival. Suddenly, a loud announcer's voice boomed from a nearby tent.

"Step right up! Join the pie-eating contest and win a golden trophy!"

Mildred's eyes widened with excitement. "Did you hear that, Maynard? A golden trophy! This is your moment!"

Maynard hesitated, glancing at the line of contestants, all of whom looked much older and hungrier than him. "I don't know, Mildred. I'm not exactly a pie-eating expert."

Mildred neared closer, her translucent hands on her hips. "Nonsense! You'll be a legend the *Pie King* of the County Fair!"

Before Maynard could protest, Mildred had already dragged him to the registration table. Moments later, he found himself seated at a long table, a steaming cherry pie placed in front of him.

"On your mark... get set... GO!" the announcer yelled, and the crowd erupted in cheers.

Maynard hesitantly took a bite, the warm cherry filling smearing across his face. He noticed Mildred hovering behind the other contestants, her mischievous grin growing wider.

"Mildred, what are you up to now?" he mumbled through a mouthful of pie.

"Oh, nothing," she said innocently, before sneakily swiping a chunk of pie from the plate of the contestant next to Maynard. The man looked around, confused, and then glared at Maynard.

"Hey, kid, stop stealing my pie!" the man growled.

"I didn't" Maynard tried to explain, but before he could finish, Mildred had already moved on to the next contestant, stealing another bite.

One by one, the other contestants began to argue, blaming Maynard for their mysteriously disappearing pies.

"Stop it, Mildred!" Maynard whispered furiously. His face appeared as red as the cherry filling.

"I'm just helping you win!" Mildred giggled.

Determined to stop her antics, Maynard lunged to grab Mildred, forgetting she was invisible to everyone else. His sudden movement startled the contestant beside him, who accidentally flipped his pie into the air.

In the chaos that followed, Maynard lost his balance and tumbled into the table. Plates of pies went flying, landing on contestants, spectators, and even the announcer.

The tent erupted into laughter and groans as everyone wiped cherry filling off their faces. Maynard sat on the ground, covered in pie, while Mildred floated above him, clutching her side in laughter.

"You did it, Maynard! You're officially the *Pie King!*" she giggled.

"More like the *Clumsy Pie King*," Maynard muttered, wiping pie off his face as the crowd continued to laugh.

After the pie-eating fiasco, Maynard wiped the last remnants of cherry filling off his face. "I need a break," he grumbled. "Something calm, something... normal."

They left the pie eating contest area and headed toward the rides section. As they strolled past the flashing lights and noisy booths, the towering Ferris wheel caught Maynard's eye.

The slow, rhythmic motion and the promise of a peaceful view of the fair seemed like the perfect escape.

"This looks like the right ride for me," Maynard said, stepping into the line.

Mildred neared and squinted up at the massive wheel. "Oh, a giant spinning contraption! Count me in! And look, the gondolas look like colorful tea-cups!"

Maynard sighed. "Just promise me you'll behave."

"Of course!" Mildred replied with a not-so-reassuring grin.

As they climbed into one of the gondolas, Maynard sat on one side and Mildred on the other. Maynard leaned back and began taking in the sights. "What a view, Mildred," he said.

The wheel began to move, lifting them higher and higher. The fair looked magical from above, the colorful lights twinkling like stars against the night sky.

"This isn't so bad," Maynard said, finally relaxing.

Mildred, on the other hand, was anything but calm. "Maynard, look over here! You can see everything! I wonder how high we can go?"

Before Maynard could stop her, Mildred began rocking their gondola.

"Mildred! Stop!" Maynard yelled, clutching the sides of the seat.

"This is fun!" Mildred laughed, leaning out of the gondola to look down. "Hey, I can almost touch the clouds!"

The gondola swayed dangerously, and Maynard's face turned pale.

"Mildred, stop rocking! You are making me sick to my stomach!"

Suddenly, the Ferris wheel came to an abrupt halt, leaving them suspended at the very top.

"What's going on?" Maynard asked, panicked.

Mildred peered down. "Looks like a power issue... or maybe the operator needed a snack break. Either way, we're stuck!"

Maynard groaned. "This is all your fault! If you hadn't been rocking the gondola."

Mildred's playful expression faded. "I was just trying to make it fun."

"Fun? I'm stuck at the top of a Ferris wheel with an invisible ghost who thinks rules don't apply to her!"

There was a long pause before Mildred spoke again, her voice softer. "I didn't mean to ruin it for you. I guess I got carried away."

Maynard sighed, his frustration melting slightly. "Just... think before you act next time, okay?"

The two sat in silence for a moment, gazing at the fair below. From their perch, they could see everything the bustling crowd, the twinkling lights, and the faint sound of music.

"This is actually kind of nice," Maynard admitted. "It is peaceful to just sit and look at the world from up here."

Mildred smiled. "See? Sometimes being stuck isn't so bad."

The wheel began moving again, and their gondola descended to the ground.

Maynard stepped off the Ferris wheel letting out a deep breath of relief. "Solid ground," he muttered, his legs feeling a little wobbly.

"Son," said the ride operator, "May I ask you what you were doing up there? The gondola was wobbling and needed to remain still. When it wobbles, it is too dangerous to stop a ride."

"Sorry about that Mr. ride operator," said Maynard. "It will never happen again. In all my excitement of wanting to look over the edge, I accidentally stood up and caused my gondola to rock."

"Well, be more careful next time. Have a nice time at the fair," said the ride operator.

Maynard and Mildred decided it was time to find a food truck so they could purchase a caramel apple.

They approached a food stand, purchased one soft-caramel apple without nuts, and began looking for a place to sit down.

As the sun was setting over the fair, it cast hues of orange and pink in the sky. Maynard and Mildred found a quiet spot sitting next to a wooden light post.

As they looked off into the Midway, the lights of the carnival glowed brighter against the darkening sky, and the distant sounds of laughter and music filled the air.

Despite the pie-covered clothes, the near Ferris wheel disaster, and the countless mishaps, Maynard felt content.

"What a fun day today, Mildred," he said, taking a bite of his caramel apple.

Mildred neared, resting her chin on her hands. "Not bad at all. It tastes a bit sweet and sticky. So, what's next? Maybe a haunted house adventure? Or a ghostly roller coaster?"

Maynard giggled. "Let's call it a night, Mildred."

"WHEW ... Maynard, I am going to take off. Have fun explaining to your parents how pie ended up all over you. I hope the ride operator doesn't call them to tattle on you

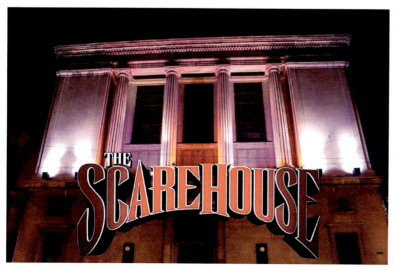

regarding Ferris wheel mishap. Enjoy the tinker toy you won at the ring toss game. And, enjoy your caramel apple.

***

"IMAGINATION"
HELPS
YOU IN YOUR
PERSONAL
GROWTH.

***

STORY 5
APPLE ORCHARD

Sunnyside Apple Orchard was known to be a popular activity destination. With its large orchard, corn maze, and pumpkin patch, one could spend hours there.

Because the orchard was so popular, Maynard's parents decided it would be best to arrive a few minutes before opening.

"WOW," he said. "Look at all the apple trees and the size of those apples! And, they even have a barnyard with animals, a tractor pulling apple carts with kids riding in them, and a ton of snack vendors."

As they got out of the car, Maynard started to shiver. "BUURRR," he said. "Where's my jacket."

The air was tinged with a hint of coolness almost stinging his face. "It sure is cold today," he observed. "Glad I wore two pairs of socks. Oh, and look, a hot chocolate stand. That will warm me up!"

Rows upon rows of apple trees stretched out before Maynard, their branches heavy with red, yellow, and green fruit. The leaves, in shades of amber, gold, and crimson, created a scene of autumn hues against the clear blue sky. The orchard was a picturesque haven—a perfect mix of nature's beauty and festive charm.

Maynard's eyes sparkled with anticipation as he passed by several treat vendors wandering over to the hay bale tug-of-war area. "Boy, that sure looks hard to do," he commented. "I'll have to pass on that one."

Today, he was determined to pick the juiciest apples and learn all about the secrets of the orchard. His heart raced with excitement for a day of exploration, fun, and hands-on learning about nature.

Just as he stepped forward, Mildred neared whispering into his ear.

"Hello Maynard," she said.

"Holy apple Mildred," he mumbled. "What are you doing here? I am going to get a bag and pick some of my mom's favorite apples. She loves to bake pies."

"Sounds delicious Maynard," said Mildred. "Let me tag along so I can help you pick the best apples."

"No, no, no," said Maynard. "Mildred, just don't shake too many apples in the trees. I plan to pick one bag full, not a wagon full."

"No problem, Maynard," she said. "Look Maynard, there is a big apple tree over there with big red apples. Let's go over and select a few good ones."

Maynard was eager to pick some of the biggest red apples in the orchard.

As he walked down a long stretch of apple trees, it felt he was walking for miles.

"Geezz, Mildred," as Maynard puffed. "Let's stop already. I see a lot of apple trees with BIG apples. Let's stop here."

Maynard took a moment to catch his breath. As he stood calmly looking up at one of the apple trees, he realized the ONE apple he really wanted to pick for his mother, the grand apple of them all, was at the top and too high for him to reach.

"Geezz, Mildred," he said. "That's the perfect red apple for my mom but I can't reach it."

"Maynard, why don't you just shake the tree and it will fall down," Mildred commented.

"Mildred," Maynard shouted. "You are not supposed to shake the apple trees. They are delicate and you could risk their growing progress."

"No one is watching Maynard," she said. "Just shake it."

Just as Maynard was about to shake the tree, an orchard caretaker neared the area with a small group of people surrounding him.

"Welcome, everyone! Today, you'll learn the art of apple picking," he announced, handing out small baskets and offering instructions on how to choose the juiciest apples.

"And over here," the caretaker said. "Look at the size of these apples!"

The caretaker continued, "You will see several varieties of apples. Notice their different colors. It takes a lot of loving care to keep them growing like year after year. One disturbing movement and the tree could perish."

"Mr. caretaker," Maynard said. "I would like to get that really BIG red apple at the top of the tree."

"That one will have to fall down on its own," as the caretaker examined the tree and noticed how high it was.

"Let me remind everyone," he said. "IF you see an apple really high, do not shake the tree. Let mother nature allow it to fall to the ground on its own."

"Rabbits," said Maynard.

"Did you say something Maynard," said the caretaker.

"AH, no sir," Maynard commented. "I must have stepped on a rotten apple that fell to the ground. Sorry about that. I'll be careful when I start picking."

Maynard immediately set to work, carefully examining each branch before gently plucking a perfect, red apple from a tree.

"This is amazing," he thought, his heart swelling with pride as he filled his basket.

"What about this one, Maynard," Mildred commented.

Meanwhile, Mildred hovered near the top of the apple tree where Maynard spotted his choice apple, she said, "Maynard, stand back and I'll shake this one off for you."

"Mildred, you know we are not supposed to shake the tree," Maynard shouted.

"I think these trees are whispering secret recipes for the best apple pie ever! And, it tells me, shake this BIG red one at the top of the tree!" Her playful banter made Maynard glance up, half-amused and half-annoyed.

"LOOK everyone ... Look at the size of my apple," shouted an apple picker nearby. "WOW!"

As the orchard participants moved from tree to tree, they exchanged lighthearted remarks about their finds. "I got the biggest apple ever!" someone shouted.

"Let me compare mine to yours," shouted a participant. "You lose, its obvious MINE is the biggest apple."

Amidst the friendly chatter and gentle teasing among participants, the afternoon began to unfold into a hint of darkness.

"Oh dear," said Maynard. "I have a few nice apples in my basket but not the one I really want. I need that BIG red apple on top of that tree."

As Maynard continued diligently picking apples from the trees, Mildred's playful curiosity got the better of her. She hovered

over the top of the tree with the BIG red apple, couldn't resist, and gave it a tug.

"Look out, Maynard! Here comes your BIG red apple!" she giggled mischievously.

Before Maynard could tell her to not shake the apple tree, the branch gave way to many apples with a soft crack, sending a cascade of shiny red apples tumbling from the tree.

In an instant, what started as a single apple became a mini "apple avalanche." Apples rained down, bouncing off the ground, and one or two even ricocheted off Maynard's head and shoulders, leaving him momentarily stunned.

A scream let out from the participants. Some teased, "Look mommy, that boy is getting an apple shower!" while others clapped in delight at the unexpected spectacle.

The orchard caretaker, who had been overseeing the harvest, shook his head in horrified disbelief as he watched the chaos unfold.

Mildred, unable to contain her amusement, neared Maynard and remarked, "Well, it looks to me you are bringing home several baskets of apples today! Oh, ... and here's that BIG red apple you wanted."

Maynard's face burned red with embarrassment. Determined not to let the mishap ruin the day, he scrambled to gather as many fallen apples as he could before the orchard caretaker came over to him.

"Hello young man," said the caretaker. "What happened here?"

"I'm sorry Mr. orchard caretaker," Maynard said apologetically. "I was picking apples from this tree and I must have slipped on these bad apples on the ground and bumped up against the tree."

"Remember," the caretaker advised in a warm, steady tone, "careful harvesting not only preserves the quality of the fruit but also shows respect for nature's bounty."

"I must say, Maynard," Mildred teased as she handed him the BIG red apple he wanted, "you need to be happy with your pickings and know your mother will be happy with whatever you bring home to her."

As the final apple was placed in his basket, the caretaker nodded approvingly. "Well done, everyone. Sometimes, even a little chaos can lead to a valuable lesson. Be kind to apple trees as they will be kind back to you."

As the day's adventures wound down, Maynard found a quiet spot beneath a towering apple tree. The sun was dipping low, casting a golden glow over the orchard.

Leaning against the tree trunk, Maynard reflected on the day's chaos and triumphs. He realized that persistence, careful observation, and teamwork were just as valuable as the perfect harvest.

"Even if things didn't turn out the way I anticipated, the process of patience was my rewarding lesson," he thought.

Mildred neared pointing to a GREEN apple. "Maynard, do you see that GREEN apple on the branch over there? All it needs is time to turn into a big RED apple. Sometimes, a little restraint leads to better results."

She paused, her eyes twinkling. "Your determination to pick that BIG red apple turned our mishap into a success."

"How so Mildred," said Maynard. "You almost got me yelled at from the orchard caretaker and banned from the apple orchard."

"Did you notice when the apples fell on top of you that everyone pitched in to remove the fallen ones from the ground putting them into their baskets? People cared about those apples and didn't want to see them left on the ground to decay."

"I suppose you have a point," mumbled Maynard.

"Okay everyone," shouted the orchard caretaker. "That will do it for today. Please bring your apples to the clerks so they can get weighed and paid for. Thanks for supporting Sunnyside Apple Orchard."

"WHEW," said Mildred. "I think I am going to take off. Have fun dragging your four bags of apples home. Don't lie to your mom when you tell her how you managed to get that really BIG one from the top of a tree. Hope the tree wasn't too traumatized by it being shaken. And, next time, let's go to another orchard to pick other varieties of apples."

Maynard carried four bags of apples home to his mother.

"What on earth," his mother commented. "Maynard, how many apples did you pick today? Good grief, we certainly can't eat these many apples in a week."

"Look Mom!" Maynard shouted as he held up the BIG red apple. "I picked this really big one just for you."

"Oh Maynard," his mother commented. "It's a pretty apple and certainly is a big one. Let's cut it up to share amongst myself, you, and your father." Together, they shared the apple.

As they were enjoying the apple, his mother asked, "Dear, how did you get that bump on your head?"

***

"IMAGINATION"
HELPS
YOU BECOME MORE
FOCUSED IN
COMPLICATED
SITUATIONS.

***

STORY 6
OUTDOOR SCAVENGER HUNT

Each year, Springhaven Park, located just a few miles from the outskirts of Maynard's town, holds an annual seek-and-find scavenger hunt, bringing many people to the event.

Festive banners, twinkling lights, and colorful autumn decorations adorn every corner of the park, creating an atmosphere of excited anticipation. Who will find and win the *Golden Dusty* medallion this year?

As the crowd buzzes with excitement, an announcement echoes through the park: "Hello ladies and gentlemen, boys and girls, the 6th annual scavenger hunt is about to begin!" shouted the organizer. "This event is unique this year, it promises a bit of adventure and a chance to win the *Golden Dusty* medallion.

"The Golden Dusty," Maynard mumbled. "WOW!"

Maynard's eyes lit up with determination as he stood among several awaiting the whistle to blow. He had always dreamed of proving his detective skills and today felt like the perfect opportunity.

Clutching a small notepad and pen, Maynard resolved to leave no clue unexamined. "This is my chance," he thought, his heart pounding with a mix of excitement and nerves.

Just as the hunt was about to begin, Mildred appeared. Her translucent form shimmered in the sunlight.

"Hello Maynard," she whispered. "Are you ready to find the Golden Dusty?" she teased, a playful glint in her eye.

"Holy medallion, Mildred," Maynard shouted. "What are you doing here? I am about to set out to find the *Golden Dusty* medallion. I can't have you tagging along bugging me. Besides, I am determined to win this year!"

"Oh Maynard," said Mildred. "What's the harm in having me throw you a few clues?"

"Mildred, this event requires skill. And, your giving me clues to find the *Golden Dusty* would be cheating," Maynard said with conviction and honesty.

Maynard sighed, half-amused and half-exasperated. "I'm serious about this, Mildred. I want to win!"

Mildred grinned. "Well, I have a few clues up my sleeve that might just lead you into an unpredictable adventure!"

With that, the curious invitation to the scavenger hunt marked the beginning of a day full of mystery, laughter, and unexpected fun.

As the crowd gathered near the outdoor rotunda, centered in the middle of the park, the organizer stepped forward to explain the scavenger hunt rules.

With a friendly smile, he handed out envelopes containing the first clue to each participant. "Remember, the clues are a bit scrambled," said the organizer. "Work alone and let your imagination lead you to the *Golden Dusty* medallion. Good luck!"

Maynard eagerly tore open his envelope and pulled out a neatly folded piece of paper. He quickly scribbled the first clue into his notebook with determination etched on his face. The clue read: "A wooden stick made into a pencil creates a perfect pairing." Though mysterious, its interesting wording set the tone for the day's adventure.

Mildred neared Maynard and began interpreting the clue into his ear. "Let's break this down, Maynard."

"Maynard, what type of wooden stick? Branch from a tree, lumber, already made chair?" questioned Mildred.

"Mildred, be quiet," remarked Maynard. "I'm thinking. I bet the next clue can be found in a place that has trees. They are made from wood."

"After all," he said, "This is an outdoor scavenger hunt, so, the next clue must be outside somewhere."

A sense of urgency began to build. The clock was ticking, and every minute felt like a race against time.

Their playful banter turned into rapid-fire exchanges as frustration set in when clue after clue seemed to lead them in circles. "This is getting ridiculous," Maynard muttered, glancing at his watch. Mildred, with her usual mischievous grin, replied, "Maybe the universe is trying to tell us something!"

Just then, the pair unexpectedly bumped into an enthusiastic scavenger hunter. "Hey, slowpoke!" the rival teased. "Did you lose your scavenger map? Looks to me like you have been walking in circles. Ha-ha-ha."

"Just ignore him, Maynard," Mildred said. "If he was so good at this, he would have found the *Golden Dusty* by now."

Amid the chaos, it was the last clue that clicked his thoughts and reasoning into place.

"I think I have figured this out, Mildred," Maynard whispered with excitement.

As Maynard re-read his notes in his notebook, the pieces of the puzzle suddenly fell into order. "Wait a minute..." he exclaimed, his eyes lighting up with realization. Mildred, ever alert, darted forward. "That's it! The final location is right by the art museum!"

Their hearts pounded as they quickened their pace toward the designated spot. The tension, once mounting in frustration, transformed into a surge of excitement and anticipation.

Every step felt like the culmination of their persistent efforts.

In that charged moment, the duo braced themselves to uncover the mystery, bringing them to a place directly behind the *Olivia Wood* statue. *Olivia Wood* was known for writing enlightening poetry.

Maynard and Mildred believed the final clue awaited them at this statue. But first, before walking in that direction, they needed to find a quiet location to spread out their clues to be certain they were not being lured to the wrong place.

As they arranged the clues in the correct order, a clear picture emerged: all signs pointed to a hidden box behind the *Olivia Wood* statue.

Their excitement surged as Maynard whispered out loud, "There is no doubt in my mind Mildred, that we've got this!" Mildred nodded eagerly, her ghostly form buzzing with anticipation.

While other participants were roaming the area, they quietly snuck behind objects making their way to the *Olivia Wood* statue. Their hearts pounded in unison.

"Look Mildred, I see a blue folded note tucked inside that flower plant over there!" shouted Maynard. "I just know we found the *Golden Dusty* medallion!"

"A man is heading in our direction. GRAB THE CLUE, Maynard," shouted Mildred.

"I have it!! I am opening the note!" shouted Maynard.

As others gathered around, some stood with curiosity while others seemed disappointed.

"READ THE NOTE!" someone screamed out loud. "Boy, did you win the *GOLDEN DUSTY?*"

Maynard opened the note.

The note read: "I am sorry. You have worked very hard to get here. There was a mix-up—the *Golden Dusty* was moved to another location as hiding it here was against city rules. It was too late to gather all the clues for this event. Keep looking."

"Keep looking?!" said Maynard.

Just as he finished reading the note, the onlookers scattered. "There is still time to find the *Golden Dusty*," one shouted.

Maynard and Mildred exchanged amused glances as the note explained the misunderstanding. "Well, it seems we solved nothing Mildred."

Suddenly, they heard a loud commotion in the background. Clapping and screaming. "I FOUND IT, I FOUND IT!" shouted a participant.

The *Golden Dusty* medallion was found near a small bird feeder just two blocks away. People were congratulating the finder while others were walking away.

Maynard began shaking his head in disappointment.

"Cheer up, Maynard," said Mildred. "Better luck next year."

After the mystery in finding the *Golden Dusty* was solved, the excitement of the scavenger hunt began to settle into a quiet, reflective calm.

Maynard sat down by a tree adorned with golden leaves. Mildred sat beside him.

He took a moment to reflect on the day's adventure.

"Today, I learned that persistence, determination, and careful observation are just as important as winning any prize," he said.

"Maynard," said Mildred, "Your determination and focus were essential in being part of the scavenger hunt. This event gave you a chance to practice a few skills, learn, and grow. I'm really proud of you."

"WHEW," said Mildred. "Maynard, I am going to take off. Have fun finding your way home. I hope you can recover from all the effort you put into trying to find the *Golden Dusty*. Sometimes, the smallest adventures are the ones that bring great excitement and memorable lessons."

***

"IMAGINATION"
HELPS
YOU BECOME MORE
CREATIVE.

***

STORY 7
MAKING A SCARECROW

Nothing indicates the sense of the Fall season more than a crisp autumn feel in the morning. The sun shining brightly through the clouds carries with it a gentle, cool breeze hinting Winter is approaching.

A patchwork of red, orange, and yellow leaves covering a browning lawn prepares itself for a long Winter. The morning dew pushing noticeable smells of wet dirt, pumpkins, and hay into the air creating the perfect scent for a school field trip.

It was late October when Maynard's 5th grade class embarked on a field trip to Clan Benson's Farm. The students buzzed with excitement as they hopped on and off the school bus rushing toward the front gate of the pumpkin farm.

Mr. Delpworth, who joined the class on the field trip, greeted the friendly farm owner at the gate with a broad smile.

"Alright class!" Mr. Delpworth shouted. "Be on your best behavior. Today, we will be participating in Clan Benson's Farm scarecrow-building contest! He needs our help to create interesting scarecrows for all the people that come here for the season."

Maynard's heart raced with a mix of excitement and nerves. He wanted to make the most interesting scarecrow but had never built one before.

"Everyone, come on over here to this barn. Mr. Benson has prepared for us all the materials we need to create our scarecrows!" Mr. Delpworth shouted.

"Hello Maynard," whispered Mildred.

"Holy scarecrow Mildred," Maynard shouted. "What are you doing here? I am about to create the best scarecrow in my class!"

Mildred neared closer, her translucent form flickering in the sunlight. "Ooooh, this is going to be fun!" she whispered. "We should make ours extra spooky!"

Maynard groaned. Mildred's idea of "helping" usually led to chaos, but there was no stopping her once she got excited.

"No, no, no," mumbled Maynard. "We are supposed to work independently to create the best-looking scarecrow. I can't have you helping me."

"Did you have a question, Maynard?" asked Mr. Delpworth.

"Just remember class, there should be no talking while Mr. Benson is trying to demonstrate to us how to create a scarecrow," Mr. Delpworth said as a reminder.

Mr. Delpworth, on the instruction of Mr. Benson, put the students in groups of three to share in the supplies handed out: old clothes, bundles of straw, wooden frames, and a box full of accessories.

Maynard was grouped with Emma, a creative classmate known for her artistic touch, and Oliver, a younger boy determined to prove himself.

As they examined their materials, Mildred neared and whispered into Maynard's ear, "Let's give our scarecrow a superhero cape! Or what about glowing eyes?"

"Good idea, Mildred," said Maynard.

"Maynard, who is Mildred? Don't you know my name by now – its Emma!" she remarked.

"Oh, sorry, Emma," he commented. "That was just a slip."

Emma rolled her eyes. "Maynard, don't tell us what your idea is – this is supposed to be a contest."

Oliver nodded. "Yeah, what is the fun of making these things if we can't reveal our scarecrow ideas as a bit of a surprise!"

Maynard felt caught between the idea of creating a superhero or scary monster. He wanted to win, but he also wanted to make sure their scarecrow didn't end up looking ridiculous.

As the students got to work stuffing straw into the old clothes, some of their efforts didn't go as planned.

The straw kept falling out, leaving trails around their feet. Oliver tried hammering a wooden frame together but ended up knocking over their supplies into a pile.

Emma tried to put artistic touches on her scarecrow only to have one ponytail end up longer than the other.

Mildred, eager to speed things up, whispered suggestions that only Maynard could hear. "Just float the straw in, easy peasy!" Maynard sighed. "We can't cheat, Mildred."

Meanwhile, other groups were making significant progress. The group next to them had already dressed their scarecrow in a checkered shirt and overalls.

Another team was giving their scarecrow a pirate hat and an eye patch. Maynard's anxiety grew heavier as he watched the others make significant progress while he was falling further behind in his efforts.

Seeing Maynard struggle, Mildred decided to take matters into her own hands. "Just a little boost to help him!" she whispered as she waved her translucent fingers toward Maynard's scarecrow.

Instantly, straw flew into the scarecrow's clothes. However, she overdid it and the scarecrow swelled up like a balloon, looking more like a stuffed turkey than a spooky figure.

Maynard couldn't help but notice that the scarecrow was about to burst.

"BOOM" – the scarecrow exploded with straw flying everywhere. The students screamed.

"Here Maynard," said Mildred. "Let me add a final touch!" Mildred picked up a hat from the supplies pile and soared it across the barn landing on top of Maynard's scarecrow.

Thinking the incident was a strong gust of wind, the students initially gasped and then, in unison, burst into laughter.

Maynard groaned. "Not again!"

"I think your scarecrow looks like a crazy hay monster!" laughed Oliver.

"Put a little lipstick on it and it could be a princess monster," giggled Emma.

Maynard looked at his scarecrow and couldn't quite figure out why it looked like such a mess.

"Here Maynard, let me help straighten some of that up," she said. "After all, it just needs a little tuck here and a straightening there."

Oliver couldn't help but notice Maynard's attempt and started laughing and pointing. "Look everyone, his scarecrow looks like a fisherman not a superhero!"

"I don't like the way they are making fun of your work Maynard," Mildred said. "Here let me teach them a lesson."

"Mildred, stay out of it," said Maynard. "I don't care if they want to make fun of my scarecrow."

"Making fun is not nice," whispered Mildred. "Let me help Emma and Oliver out to give them a taste of their own medicine!"

Mildred started reconfiguring the works of Emma and Oliver.

"HOW ABOUT A LITTLE LIPSTICK on your scarecrow, EMMA!" Mildred silently shouted.

"Where did that lipstick come from? I think my scarecrow is bleeding from its mouth!" shouted Emma.

"And, OLIVER, I've never seen a pirate with straw legs before. How about I twist one of his legs over his head!" Mildred said rebelliously.

"How did that leg get twisted around its head?" said puzzled Oliver.

Other classmates noticed Maynard struggling to put his scarecrow back in order.

"Why are you so upset?" asked Mildred. "It just needs a little help, that's all."

Others, including Emma and Oliver, noticed Maynard becoming upset. They stopped what they were doing, gathered near him, and helped him to recreate his scarecrow into a superhero.

They gave it wild, spiky hair, a goofy stitched-on smile, and Oliver found a pair of oversized sunglasses to complete the look. It was wacky, but it had personality.

By the time they finished, their scarecrow looked like something out of a cartoon—silly, funny, and creative.

When it was time for the judging, Mr. Delpworth walked around, inspecting each scarecrow. Some were tall and traditional; others were pirate or superhero themed. Then he studied Maynard's scarecrow.

"Well, this is certainly unique!" he said, chuckling. "I've never seen a scarecrow quite like this before. What is it?"

"Mr. Delpworth, my scarecrow is called *Super Hex Man!*" he shouted. "It is my special superhero creation!"

"Very impressive, Maynard," the teacher commented.

As the results were announced, Maynard did not receive first place. However, he did receive a special award: "Most Creative Superhero."

Maynard felt a wave of relief and happiness. "Mildred, we didn't win first place but at least we still won something."

"WHEW, Maynard, ... I think I am going to take off," said Mildred. "Have fun brushing hay out of your hair and off your clothes. I know it wasn't very nice rubbing red lipstick all over Emma's scarecrow but it did give it some character. And, as for Oliver's scarecrow, maybe his should be a contortionist rather than a pirate ... that's a new one."

Each student took turns getting a photo of themselves in front of their scarecrows. Maynard stood proud of his superhero scarecrow, "Super Hex Man."

STORY 8
TRICK OR TREAT

STORY 8
TRICK OR TREAT

Halloween night was one of Maynard's favorite outdoor activities in October.

The air was crisp and carried the unmistakable scent of decaying autumn leaves.

"See yah later, Mom and Dad," Maynard shouted, as he put on his sneakers. He pulled his homemade ghost sheet over his head, adjusted the strap to his candy bag, and grabbed a candy bucket.

With a wide grin, he marched out of the house into the darkness. His white sheet-turned-ghost-costume swaying slightly in the breeze.

As he walked on the grass in his yard, fallen leaves that turned brittle crunched beneath his feet.

"I just LOVE trick and treating. I can't wait to get this whole bucket filled with candy," Maynard said enthusiastically.

Suddenly, a familiar voice echoed behind him. "Hello, Maynard."

Maynard froze, almost dropping his bag onto the sidewalk.

"Holy candy bag, Mildred!" he exclaimed, spinning around. "What are you doing here?" Maynard asked, half-accusingly. "You'll scare all the trick-or-treaters away!"

Mildred shrugged nonchalantly. "Doubtful," she said.

"Maynard, this is my favorite time of year. I can get away with pulling tricks on people, and my mischief goes completely unnoticed," Mildred cackled gleefully. "By the way, what exactly are you supposed to be?"

Maynard puffed up his chest proudly. "I'm a GHOST! Want to know how I made my costume?"

Mildred raised an eyebrow. "Not really."

"Well, I took a sheet from my bed, cut two holes for eyes, and threw the whole thing over myself." He spread his arms wide, the sheet fluttering slightly. "BOO! I'm a GHOST!"

Mildred could hardly contain her laughter. "S-c-a-r-y? Not."

Maynard frowned as he adjusted the sheet to make himself look scarier. "You don't know anything about Halloween, Mildred. This costume is a classic!"

"You know, Maynard," she began, "Halloween is the best time of year."

"Oh, how so, Mildred?" asked Maynard.

"Tricks are more fun than getting treats," said Mildred.

"I'm in it for the candy, Mildred," said Maynard. "Besides, I can fill up my bag and eat candy forever."

"Or until you get sick, Maynard," said Mildred.

"Besides," Mildred smirked. "Candy is overrated. Tricks are timeless. And, with a costume like yours, Maynard, you could benefit from a little help."

"What's wrong with my costume?" Maynard demanded, as he clutched the edges of his sheet.

"Oh, nothing," Mildred said, her tone dripped with sarcasm. "It's just... well, it's not exactly 'ghostly.' More like a sad bedsheet with worn out holes in it."

"Mildred, be quiet, before we go to the first house, I need to practice my lines," commented Maynard.

"Hit me with it!" said Mildred.

"Ah, Ha-Hmmm," Maynard cleared his throat. "Trick or treat."

His voice was flat and unconvincing.

Mildred burst into laughter. "Oh, come on, Maynard! That's not going to scare anyone. You're supposed to be a scary ghost, not a bored librarian."

93

"Well, how would you say it?" Maynard challenged.

Mildred leaned in close, her eyes glinting with mischief. "Like this." She threw back her head and let out an eerie wail.

"TRICK OR TREAT!" Her voice echoed, sending a shiver down Maynard's spine.

"That's... actually kind of creepy," Maynard remarked.

"Thank you," Mildred said with a mock bow. "Now, let me help you. Open your mouth wider. No, wider. Wider! There we go." She yanked at the edges of his mouth, pulling his lips downward.

"Hey! Stop that!" Maynard protested, batting her hands away. "How am I supposed to be scary with my face all messed up?"

"You'll figure it out," Mildred said with a chuckle. "Deal with it. You've got the whole night ahead of you to practice!"

Maynard and Mildred continued walking down the sidewalk noticing older homes. Some of them were well kept, the others had broken windows and loose shutters.

"WOW ... cool. This block really knows how to get into the spirit of Halloween. All these houses look creepy and scary! Let's stop at this first one," said Maynard.

Maynard hesitated as he walked up several cement steps to approach the first house. He clutched his candy bag tightly. The mailbox stood crooked on the corner of the yard. The name was etched in bold, jagged letters: *Frank-N-Stein*.

"That's got to be a joke, right? The person who lives here sure knows how to set the mood," Maynard whispered. "Look Mildred, the mailbox is decorated for a Halloween mood. Cool!"

"Oh brother," Mildred commented.

The house gave off an eerie feeling. The shutters hung crooked and a dim, flickering porch light casted odd shadows.

A chill breeze carried the faint sound of creaking hinges. Maynard shivered.

"I'm afraid to walk up to the door," he muttered, stepping cautiously onto the creaky wooden porch.

"Oh, come on!" Mildred said, nudging him forward. "This is exactly what Halloween is about … spooky houses and weird neighbors. Go on, knock!"

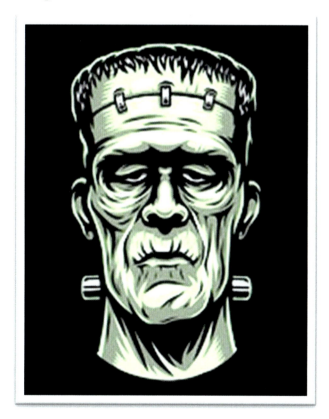

Summoning his courage, Maynard rapped on the door.

KNOCK-KNOCK-KNOCK.

The creaking sound grew louder as the door slowly swung open, revealing a hulking figure in the doorway. He was tall, broad, and had a greenish hue to his skin. Bolts stuck out from either side of his neck, and his expression was blank but intimidating.

"Uh… trick or treat?" Maynard said hesitantly.

"Here Maynard, hold my bucket. We got this," shouted Mildred. "Trick or treat!" Mildred echoed loudly.

"Stop that!" Maynard whispered, glaring at Mildred. "I mean, sir, trick or treat. Uh… nice costume, by the way!"

The figure tilted his head slightly, his heavy brow furrowing.

"Wait…" Maynard said, leaning closer. "That's not a costume!" Before the figure could respond, Mildred tugged at Maynard's sleeve. "Quick Maynard, Look Over There!"

Maynard turned to see a jack-o-lantern floating in mid-air, its carved grin glowing eerily.

"That's a cool trick!" Maynard said nervously to Mr. Stein, trying to mask his unease. "The jack-o-lantern is floating in the air! COOL!"

The figure in the doorway remained silent, his eyes fixed on Maynard. The pumpkin hovered in the air.

"*Scary*," said Mildred. "Look Maynard, there are two of them!"

"Two of them?!" shouted Maynard. "What, you mean, the floating jack-o-lantern wasn't a trick!" Maynard stood in confusion, his voice crackling.

"Maybe they are twins!" Mildred giggled.

"Mildred, you must be out of your mind. If they *were twins*, don't you think they would look the same?" commented Maynard.

"Oh, sorry, … Mr. Frank-N-Stein, are you asking me what I am? Well, I'm a GHOST!" Maynard blurted out with confidence.

"How insulting," Mildred smirked.

Suddenly, the door slammed shut with a loud bang! Maynard jumped back nearly dropping his candy bucket.

"Wait! Don't shut the door! You didn't give me my candy!" Maynard protested, banging on the door again.

Mildred neared him, smirking. "Well, that went well."

"Now look at what you have done!" Maynard snapped. "You scared away both Mr. Frank-N-Steins. And, I have no candy in my bag!"

"Or maybe they didn't like your costume," Mildred said with a shrug. "What a pity. He-he-he."

"Come on, Maynard," said Mildred. "There are 20 more houses on this block. If you are lucky, you might get half of your bucket filled up by midnight. And, watch out for those scary goblins."

"Goblins, what goblins," Maynard shrieked. "WAIT, Mildred don't leave me. What am I saying?"

Mildred let out a spooky chuckle, swirling around him like a playful mist.

"WHEW, Maynard, I am going to take off," Mildred whispered. "Once this night is over, I would sure hate to see your dental bill."

Maynard continued to fumble his way down the street to a few more houses before calling it quits for the night. His candy in his bucket filled the rim.

As predicted, he ate too much candy and ended up in the emergency room getting lectured by the doctor. "Maynard," the doctor said, "We all get excited eating lots of candy on Halloween but we still need to be mindful of our health."

As Maynard lay in bed that evening, he thought about all the houses he went to and how each one had a different feeling about them.

He especially remembered the Frankenstein house. "Gosh, that man looked so real," he mumbled out loud to himself. "Maybe, just maybe, he is Frankenstein!"

"Maynard," shouted his mother. "Stop talking to yourself and go to sleep. You know the doctor wants you to get some rest after inhaling all that candy."

"Eyes are closed, Mom," he shouted.

"Maybe I'll have to do some detective work to figure out if that man is the real Frankenstein. After all, ... if Mildred is real in my mind ... then, Frankenstein is more than likely ... also real.

***

"IMAGINATION"
HELPS
YOU BECOME MORE
CONFIDENT.

***

"DEADWARD"
WRAPPING UP

GOOD EVENING ... BLAHH ...

I am DEADWARD ... the Count of Transylvania.
Have you enjoyed reading the Fall Stories in this book?

That Halloween candy sure looked tempting.

My favorite are red-colored hard candies. I eat them when I
need to get some rest. Red makes me very, very sleepy. My
best resting position is lying upside down. Ahhh, relaxing.

I see you met my long-distance cousin, Franky.

Franky and I used to go trick or treating in our community a
long time ago.

We would go house to house. When the owner opened the
door, I would say, "BLAHHH" and Franky would say, "AHG".
He had a bit of a speech issue.

The homeowner would comment on how they loved our
costumes. We would say, "What costumes?"

They would scream, look shocked, and close their doors very
fast. We would pound on their doors asking for our candy.
Then, they would open the door and throw it at us. That was a
fun game. I would fly around catching all the candies hurling in
the air.

Did you know this book is a four-part series being produced
into short films? Be sure and read the other three books.
Check them out on the last pages. BLAHHH.

MEMORIES

- Exploration
- Fun
- Determination
- Confidence
- Common Sense

***

"IMAGINATION"
HELPS
YOU IN YOUR
SOCIAL
DEVELOPMENT.

***

ENDING
FALL MEMORIES

Field Trip
Nature
Farm

Baking
Class

Amusement
Park

County
Fair

Apple
Orchard

Outdoor
Scavenger
Hunt

Making A
Scarecrow

Trick or
Treat

NARRATORS

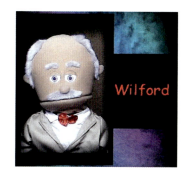
Wilford

Crazy Melmo

Deadward

***

"IMAGINATION"
HELPS
YOU EXPLORE
ALTERNATIVES.

***

[MAYNARD]   Mildred, do you remember when we went on that field trip to the nature farm?

[MILDRED]   I remember Maynard. How Romantical.

[MAYNARD]   Mildred, how about I bake for you a batch of my chocolate chip cookies.

[MILDRED]   Maynard, say something dreamy to me.

[MAYNARD]	Do you remember when I tried to pick that HUGE apple from that tall tree? It was the size of a basketball!
[MILDRED]	Boys. Such an imagination.

[MILDRED]   I remember Maynard ... I shook the tree for you and created an apple avalanche.

[MAYNARD]   Mildred, you need to learn to be kinder to the trees – they are delicate and have feelings. That HUGE apple tasted REALLY good!

[MILDRED]   Maynard, what about the time we made that scarecrow for that farm?

[MAYNARD]   My superhero scarecrow should have won. Emma never did like the red lipstick on hers.

Maynard and Mildred would share brief moments together. There were times when he would find himself in need of guidance and wanting Mildred to help him focus. Because of Mildred, Maynard learned how to trust, to care, to be less distracted, and become more focused. Her influences allowed him to explore closeness, social connection, and his own emotions. *Besties*, they will always be. I "heart" Mildred.

***

"IMAGINATION"
HELPS
IN
SOCIAL
DEVELOPMENT
SKILLS.

***

Book Series
Being Produced into Films

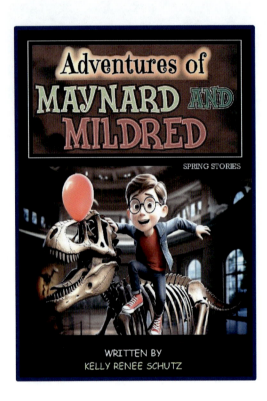

**Launched on Amazon
February 2025**

Spring Adventure Stories
Moving Again
Maynard Meets Mildred
Library
Bowling Alley
Soda Shop
Movie Theater
At the Museum
Thru the Cemetery

**Launched on Amazon
March 2025**

Summer Adventure Stories
At the Lake
Bike Ride
Campfire Fort
Hot Dog Eating Contest
Dentist
Barber Shop
Detective
At the Zoo

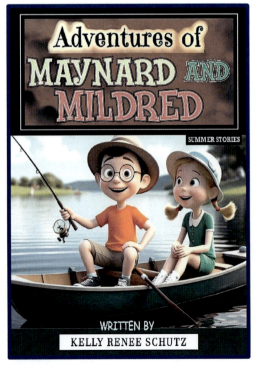

Book Series
Being Produced into Films

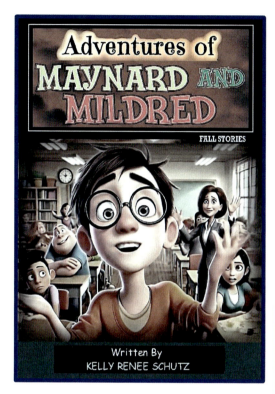

Launched on Amazon
May 2025

Fall Adventure Stories
Field Trip Nature Farm
Baking Class
Amusement Park
County Fair
Apple Orchard
Outdoor Scavenger Hunt
Making a Scarecrow
Trick or Treat

Launched on Amazon
April 2025

Winter Adventure Stories
Building a Snowman
Caroling
Santa at the Mall
Ski Trip
Ice Skating
Ice Fishing
Show and Tell
Valentine's Day

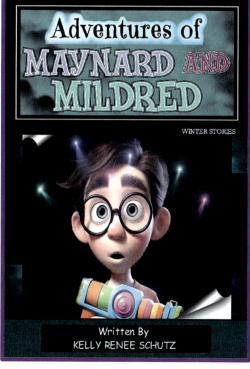

Made in the USA
Monee, IL
22 April 2025